IMAGES
of America

PENNSYLVANIA'S
COVERED BRIDGES

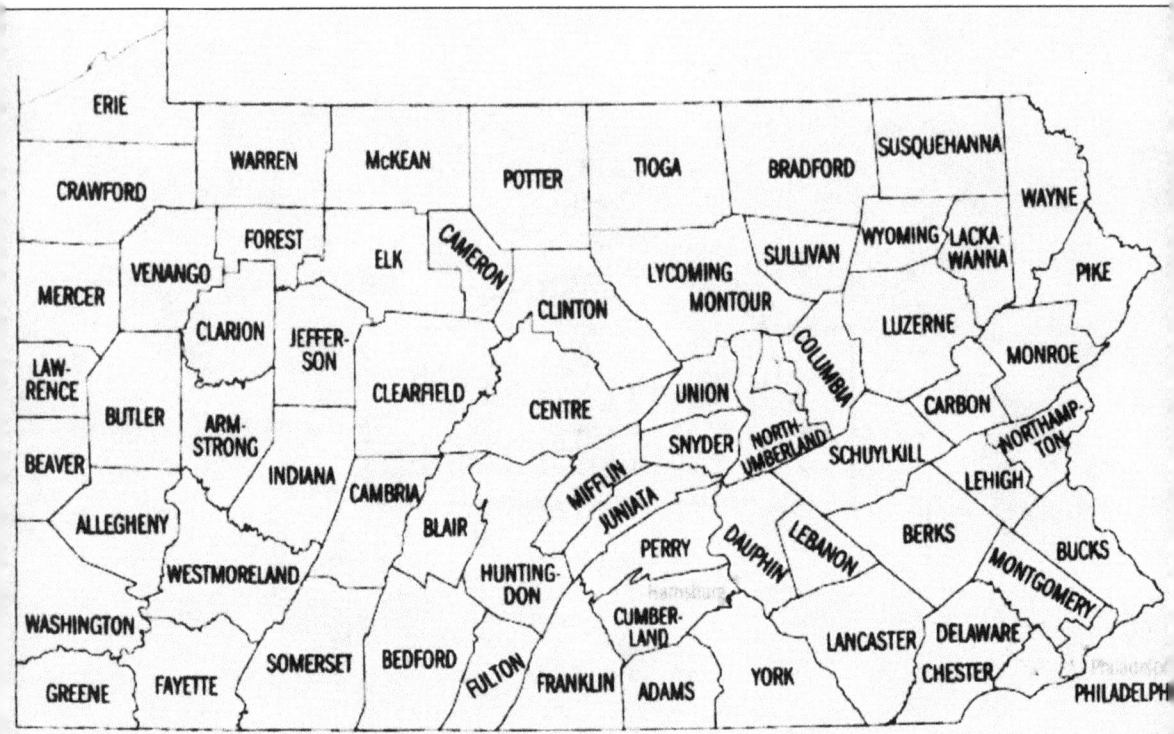

Pictured is a county map of Pennsylvania. (Author's collection.)

IMAGES
of America

PENNSYLVANIA'S
COVERED BRIDGES

Fred J. Moll

ARCADIA
PUBLISHING

Copyright © 2012 by Fred J. Moll
ISBN 978-1-5316-6249-3

Published by Arcadia Publishing
Charleston, South Carolina

Library of Congress Control Number: 2011945719

For all general information, please contact Arcadia Publishing:
Telephone 843-853-2070
Fax 843-853-0044
E-mail sales@arcadiapublishing.com
For customer service and orders:
Toll-Free 1-888-313-2665

Visit us on the Internet at www.arcadiapublishing.com

This book is dedicated to the great covered-bridge builders of the 1800s who put skill and pride in their work and left their legacy behind.

CONTENTS

ACKNOWLEDGMENTS

I would like to thank the Theodore Burr Covered Bridge Society of Pennsylvania for allowing me access to their photographs, as well as Bob and Judy Kuether for sorting through the society's photographs and assisting in the gathering of photographs for inclusion in this book. I would also like to thank Thomas E. Walczak, Thomas G. Kipphorn, Jim Smedley, and everyone else who has donated their photographs and information to the society or to me for future generations to enjoy. Gratitude goes to the Historical Society of Berks County for all the research I was able to find on Berks County's covered bridges.

INTRODUCTION

During the 1800s, there were over 12,000 covered bridges in the United States. Over the years, that number has dwindled considerably due to fire, flood, neglect, and modern replacement. Today, there are about 750 covered bridges left in the United States. In Pennsylvania, the list of covered bridges has dropped from over 1,500 in the mid-1800s to slightly over 200 today. But Pennsylvania still has more covered bridges than any other state. In fact, Pennsylvania has 25 percent of the existing covered bridges in the United States. The reason for the large abundance in Pennsylvania stems from the fact that there are many waterways that need crossing and that Pennsylvania (the name is derived from Penn's Woods) had a large number of trees in the state that provided a natural building material for the bridges. During the 1800s, Pennsylvania was almost entirely forested and was a major source of lumber for the United States.

The first covered bridge in the United States was built in Pennsylvania. Although we usually think of covered bridges as an American tradition, the idea of the covered bridge came from other continents. The earliest covered bridge on record is listed as being built in 1078 in China. Bridges were covered in order to protect the floor and truss work from the elements and thus increase the life span of the bridge. It was not until June 3, 1797, that Timothy Palmer, a bridge builder from Newburyport, Massachusetts, took out a patent for his new improvement in construction of bridges. He stressed the necessity of protecting bridges from the weather by constructing a roof over them, stating that such protection might prolong the life of a bridge from 10 or 12 years to as many as 40 years. In 1805, Timothy Palmer built America's first covered bridge in the city of Philadelphia, Pennsylvania. The bridge carried Market Street over the Schuylkill River near Thirtieth Street. Looking back, we can see that keeping a bridge dry and performing regular maintenance on it can increase its life expectancy to well over 100 years.

Pennsylvania also had the longest covered bridge ever built. The Columbia-Wrightsville Covered Bridge was constructed over the Susquehanna River and was over one mile in length. Because of Pennsylvania being the state with the most covered bridges, having the first covered bridge built in the United States, and being home to the longest covered bridge, it should be considered the "Covered Bridge Capital" of the United States.

What could have been the end to a large number of our covered bridges in Pennsylvania occurred in 1958, when the state highway department set out to modernize the highway system. In Pennsylvania, all the state-owned covered bridges were to be replaced within three years if they did not have at least a 15-ton load limit capacity, at least a 14-foot clearance, or if they had only one travel lane. This would have eliminated many of the covered bridges in Pennsylvania. There was a public outcry by local historical societies and a new group of concerned citizens, the Theodore Burr Covered Bridge Society of Pennsylvania, to save these historical structures. A meeting was setup between the state highway department and the Theodore Burr Covered Bridge Society, wherein an understanding was produced that covered bridges would try to be preserved if at all feasible. The needless destruction of these bridges slowed down, and today, the count has remained fairly constant.

Many people wonder why covered bridges were painted red. Since there were no paint companies in the early 1800s, paint had to be homemade. Red oxide of iron was a coloring pigment that was commonly found in soil. By mixing red oxide of iron, skimmed milk, lime, and linseed oil, a red paint was produced that was well suited to paint barns and covered bridges.

Most covered bridges were not toll bridges but long, expensive-to-build covered bridges, and covered bridges constructed by local bridge companies did charge toll. The smaller bridges charged about 1¢ to walk across the bridge, 6¢ to ride a horse across the bridge, and 30¢ to take a stagecoach with four horses across. The longer bridges across the Susquehanna and Delaware Rivers charged about 5¢ to walk across, 15¢ to ride a horse across, and 75¢ to take a stagecoach with four horses across. This could become expensive if a person had to cross a toll bridge daily. In most counties in Pennsylvania, a person could prepay the year's tolls in advance and save a considerable amount of toll money.

It is not known how many types of truss systems were used on all the former covered bridges of Pennsylvania, but today, there are seven types of trusses still in use on our existing covered bridges. These include the king post truss, multi-king post truss, queen post truss, Town truss, Howe truss, Smith truss, and the Burr truss. The Burr truss is the most widely used truss system today on Pennsylvania's covered bridges, with 57 percent of our existing covered bridges using the Burr truss system to support their weight and the weight of traffic going across the bridge.

The scope of this book is to look at both the past and present covered bridges of Pennsylvania. More emphasis is given to past covered bridges because historical objects are more valued once they are gone. Covered bridges are truly proud symbols of America's yesteryear. Old photographs and several old postcards provide us with a look back in time to when roads were dirt and life was simple. Various types and sizes of our past bridges are shown, from the short 27-foot-long Joe Ash Covered Bridge to the 5,390-foot-long Columbia-Wrightsville Covered Bridge. In the chapter on present covered bridges, some of the more popular existing covered bridges in the high-volume tourist areas are shown. There is also a chapter on Pennsylvania's railroad covered bridges. Most people who remembered railroad covered bridges are no longer around, and very few photographs and information exist of these structures. Finally, there is a chapter on covered bridge preservation. Over the years, covered bridges have been saved by either rebuilding them, reinforcing them, bypassing them, relocating them, or by placing safety devices on them, such as surveillance cameras, nighttime lights, sprinkler systems, and fire retardant–treated wood. Also, fines for causing damage to these bridges have been increased to deter acts of vandalism.

Historically speaking, covered bridges have been an important link in America's transportation system. Without covered bridges, our country would not have grown as quickly as it did. And of all the various types of bridges that were built, covered bridges have always been predominantly popular, stirring the most interest. Do not let covered bridges become a vanishing icon. It is up to all of us to preserve our covered bridges for future generations to enjoy.

One

PENNSYLVANIA'S PAST COVERED BRIDGES

This is the Mohrsville Covered Bridge, built in 1837 over the Schuylkill River at the village of Mohrsville, Berks County. The man in the wagon pays a toll to cross the covered bridge. The building on the right was the tollhouse. This bridge was one of 12 toll bridges in Berks County. The covered bridge was replaced in 1937. (Author's collection.)

The first covered bridge in North America was the Permanent (Market Street) Bridge. The bridge was constructed in 1805 on Market Street over the Schuylkill River in the city of Philadelphia. Timothy Palmer was the builder of the three-span Burr truss bridge, which had a length of 550 feet. The bridge got its name from the fact that there had been a temporary floating pontoon bridge at this site and that the new bridge was to be a permanent bridge. (Courtesy of the Doty collection.)

This is a rare Stereopticon slide of the Permanent (Market Street) Covered Bridge in Philadelphia. The Stereopticon viewer and slides, popular in the 1800s, were a forerunner of View-master and 3-D photographs. On November 20, 1875, the covered bridge was destroyed by fire. (Author's collection.)

This is the Lower Trenton (Bridge Street) Covered Bridge over the Delaware River from Morristown, Pennsylvania, to Trenton, New Jersey. This was the first covered bridge to be built over the Delaware River. Theodore Burr constructed the five-span covered bridge in 1805 for $180,000. After serving traffic for 71 years, the covered bridge was replaced in 1876. (Courtesy of Theodore Burr Covered Bridge Society of Pennsylvania.)

The Colossus Covered Bridge was built at Upper Ferry near the Fairmount Water Works in the city of Philadelphia. Lewis Wernwag constructed the covered bridge over the Schuylkill River during 1812 and 1813. This bridge, with a length of 340 feet, was the second longest single-span covered bridge ever built. It was destroyed by fire on September 1, 1838. (Courtesy of Theodore Burr Covered Bridge Society of Pennsylvania.)

The Eden Roller Mill (Umbel's Mill) Covered Bridge was erected over the Conestoga Creek in the village of Eden in 1848 at a cost of $1,790. The bridge connected East Lampeter and Manheim Townships in Lancaster County. In 1962, the covered bridge was replaced with a more modern structure. (Courtesy of Theodore Burr Covered Bridge Society of Pennsylvania.)

Risser's Mill (Horst's Mill) Covered Bridge was built over a branch of the Chikiswalungo (Chickies) Creek in Mount Joy Township in Lancaster County. Incidentally, the Native American word *chickeswalungo* means "the place of the crawfish." This 1872 Burr truss covered bridge was constructed by Elias McMellen, one of Lancaster's most active bridge builders. The bridge became the victim of arson on July 8, 2002. Local residents tried to have it rebuilt but to no avail. (Courtesy of Theodore Burr Covered Bridge Society of Pennsylvania.)

King's Covered Bridge was built in 1884 over the West Branch of the Octoraro Creek near Kirkwood in Lancaster County. *Octoraro* is a Native American word meaning "rushing waters." There was a previous covered bridge at this location that was erected in 1848. Elias McMellen was the builder of the 1884 Burr truss covered design, pictured here. The crossing was replaced in 1962. This photograph was taken on September 1, 1957. (Courtesy of Theodore Burr Covered Bridge Society of Pennsylvania.)

The Milton Grove Covered Bridge was constructed over Little Chikiswalungo Creek, one mile east of the town of Milton Grove, in Lancaster County. The one-span Burr truss bridge, built in 1885 by Nicholas Brown and Levi Fink, connected Ralpho and Mount Joy Townships. It was replaced in 1926. (Courtesy of Thomas G. Kipphorn.)

The Spring Grove Forge Covered Bridge was erected over the Conestoga River, a half mile south-southwest of Union Grove, in East Earl Township, Lancaster County. Elias McMellon constructed this one-span Burr truss bridge in 1874 for $3,747. The bridge was replaced in 1927. (Courtesy of Thomas G. Kipphorn.)

Johnson's Mill Covered Bridge crossed the Chikiswalungo Creek at about three-fourths of a mile northeast of Chickiesville at Marietta in Lancaster County. William Dietrich built this one-span Burr truss covered bridge in 1854 for $950. In 1867, Elias McMellen reconstructed the covered bridge for $1,650. It was destroyed by a tropical storm, originally Hurricane Agnes, on June 22, 1972. Fred J. Moll, the author of this book, took the photograph in 1968. At one time, there were over 130 covered bridges in Lancaster County. Today, less than 30 covered bridges remain. (Author's collection.)

Snavely's Mill (Second Lock) Covered Bridge was built over the Conestoga River, one mile north of New Danville, in Lancaster County. Benjamin Snavely built this 1857 two-span Burr truss covered design at a cost of $3,600. The 349-foot-long structure was located near the Second Lock of the Slackwater Canal. There were two former covered bridges at this location. The photograph was taken in September 1958. On January 20, 1968, the bridge was destroyed by fire. (Courtesy of Walter W. Pryse.)

The Wabank (Third Lock) Covered Bridge was constructed northwest of New Danville between Lancaster and Pequea Townships in Lancaster County. There was a previous bridge at this location. Jacob Huber constructed this two-span Burr truss bridge over the Conestoga River in 1841 at a cost of $2,481.82. The 246-foot-long bridge was near the Third Lock of the Slackwater Canal. The eastern span of the bridge collapsed in 1962, and the western span collapsed in 1969. (Courtesy of Walter W. Pryse.)

15

In this 1955 view of the Wabank Covered Bridge in Lancaster County, note the steep roadway approach to the bridge from the other side of the Conestoga River. (Courtesy of Chester Paes.)

Very little is known about this covered bridge other than its name. It was called the "Dummy Bridge" or the "Frankford Avenue Trolley Bridge." It was a one-span bridge that crossed the Tookany Creek in Philadelphia County near Frankford. It was shared by both trolley and roadway traffic. (Author's collection.)

The Egypt Covered Bridge was built on the southern edge of the town of Egypt in Whitehall Township in Lehigh County. The one-span Burr truss design was erected in 1850 and crossed the Coplay Creek. Note the stepped portal that was common on older wooden bridges of the Lehigh Valley. This photograph was taken on June 26, 1949. The covered bridge was demolished in 1954. (Courtesy of Theodore Burr Covered Bridge Society of Pennsylvania.)

The New Berlin Covered Bridge was located over Penns Creek at New Berlin between Union and Snyder Counties. Peter Keefer built the two-span Burr truss bridge in 1878. A flood destroyed it in 1936. This photograph shows the Snyder County portal with the town of New Berlin in the background. (Courtesy of Theodore Burr Covered Bridge Society of Pennsylvania.)

The Earlville Covered Bridge was constructed in 1852 over the Manatawny Creek between Boyertown and Yellow House in Earlville, Berks County. Both subjects on this page were built as open bridges with no roof due to a shortage of lumber. The top chord of the uncovered bridge can be seen in both bridges about three feet from the floor on the left interior. Later, the sides were raised, and roofs were installed on both these bridges. This bridge was replaced in 1938. (Author's collection.)

The Poplar Neck Covered Bridge was built in 1851 as an uncovered bridge over the Schuylkill River, located about four miles below Reading, in Berks County. About 1897, the sides were raised, and a roof was installed. This photograph was taken on January 21, 1900. The bridge was replaced in 1917. (Author's collection.)

The two-lane Douglassville Covered Bridge had elaborate stepped portals to greet its travelers. This toll bridge was erected in 1832 over the Schuylkill River at Douglassville, Berks County. The two-span Burr truss covered design had a length of 340 feet. It was washed out and rebuilt in 1850 and in 1869. This photograph was taken in on January 6, 1942. The Douglassville Covered Bridge was dismantled in 1951. (Courtesy of Walter W. Pryse.)

SCHUYLKILL RIVER & BRIDGE, HAMBURG, PA.   Pub. for Wyant's 5 & 10 Cent Store, Hamburg, Pa.

The Hamburg Covered Bridge crossed the Schuylkill River between Hamburg and West Hamburg in Berks County. This one-span Burr truss toll bridge was built in 1828 and had a length of 202 feet. The bridge was washed out by a flood in 1850 and reconstructed. In 1883, it was declared toll free. The covered bridge was replaced in 1928 with a concrete span. (Author's collection.)

The Pine Forge (Lower Bridge) Covered Bridge was built in 1834 over the Manatawny Creek in the village of Pine Forge in Douglass Township, Berks County. The bridge was sometimes called the Lower Bridge because there were two covered bridges near Pine Forge. This photograph was taken on May 27, 1938. The bridge was set on fire by vandals on Labor Day night, September 5, 1938, and burned down. (Courtesy of Walter W. Pryse.)

Jonathan Bitner constructed the Old Pine Iron Works (Upper Bridge) Covered Bridge in 1855 near the village of Pine Forge in Douglass Township, Berks County. Note the diagonal stripes that warned drivers when approaching the bridge portals and abutments. This Manatawny Creek bridge was destroyed by fire on Halloween night, October 31, 1938. (Author's collection.)

Bushong's Covered Bridge was erected in 1857 over the Tulpehocken Creek and the Union Canal, two miles north of Reading. The bridge took its name from Bushong's Paper Mill, which was located next to the bridge. Bushong's was a two-span Burr truss design that was 340 feet in length when measured from portal to portal. On March 28, 1959, it became a victim of arson and was never replaced. This photograph was taken on April 13, 1941. (Author's collection.)

Reber's Covered Bridge was constructed in 1838 between Bern and Upper Heidelberg Townships in Berks County. This one-span Burr truss covered bridge, named after Reber's Mill, crossed the Tulpehocken Creek. The remains of Reber's Mill can be seen to the right of the bridge. This span was replaced with an iron bridge in 1922. (Author's collection.)

At a cost of $31,200, Lawrence Corson built the Dekalb Street Covered Bridge in Norristown, Montgomery County, in 1829. The four-span bridge crossed the Schuylkill River and had a length of 800 feet. Note the ornamental Corinthian columns and fancy artwork on the portals. One lane was used by the trolley company, one was for regular traffic, and the middle lane was a pedestrian lane. The bridge burned down in April 1924. (Courtesy of Jim Smedley.)

Interior of DeKalb Street Bridge—Norristown, Pa.

This photograph shows the interior of the DeKalb Street Covered Bridge. On the floor, trolley tracks can be seen, and a trolley rail is on the rafters above. The space to the right would have been the pedestrian walkway in the center of the bridge. (Author's collection.)

22

Knight's (Red Hill/Markley's Mill) Covered Bridge in Montgomery County was constructed in 1835 over the Perkiomen Creek. This Town truss covered design was erected in Upper Hanover Township, six miles above Green Lane. The bridge had four spans and a length of 300 feet. (Courtesy of Theodore Burr Covered Bridge Society of Pennsylvania.)

Although Knight's Covered Bridge was repaired several times over the years, most of the timbers and wooden pegs were original, hewn from the oak trees close to the bridge. It was torn down in 1956 to make room for a water supply reservoir. This was the last standing covered bridge in Montgomery County. (Courtesy of Montgomery County Courthouse.)

A bridge company was formed in 1848 for the purpose of erecting a toll covered bridge over the Schuylkill River at Port Kennedy (Betzwood) in Montgomery County. The village of Port Kennedy was important for its lime industry during the 19th century. The covered bridge was built in 1849 and freed from toll in 1886. (Courtesy of Montgomery County Courthouse.)

The Port Kennedy Covered Bridge had four spans and was 560 feet in length. But, by 1901, the covered bridge became wobbly and developed a twist and bulge in the center. It was decided to replace the span with an iron bridge. In 1901, the old covered bridge was torn down and replaced with an iron bridge. Today, little remains of the village of Port Kennedy. This area is near Valley Forge National Historical Park. (Courtesy of Montgomery County Courthouse.)

The Schwenksville (Hunsberger's Mill) Covered Bridge was built in 1833 over the Perkiomen Creek in Montgomery County near Schwenksville. The two-span Town truss bridge had a length of 186 feet. Note how close the train tracks came to the portal of the bridge. (Courtesy of Theodore Burr Covered Bridge Society of Pennsylvania.)

The village of Schwenksville took its name from early settler Hans Michael Schwenk, who came to Pennsylvania from Germany in 1739. Note the flag flying on the flag stop railroad building in the foreground. If this flag was out, the train would stop to pick up passengers. This covered bridge was destroyed by fire on November 23, 1923. (Courtesy of Montgomery County Courthouse.)

This is a photograph of the 1868 Madison (Kennelworth) Covered Bridge across the Schuylkill River between Montgomery and Chester Counties. Note the unusual rounded portals on this Burr truss design. Very few covered bridges were built with rounded portals. The two-lane covered bridge was only in existence until 1886. (Courtesy of Theodore Burr Covered Bridge Society of Pennsylvania.)

Bridge over Brandywine, Barneston, Pa.

In this 1880s image, the Barneston Covered Bridge stretches over the East Branch of the Brandywine Creek in Chester County. The bridge was located three miles northwest of Glenmore. Robert Rigg built it in 1849 at a cost of $1,473. Originally known as Mercer's Bridge, it was a one-span burr truss design that was removed in 1950. (Courtesy of Octavia Bull.)

The Heyville Covered Bridge was on Rosemont Road between Springfield and Upper Darby Townships in Delaware County. The bridge was near the village of Heyville, which is called Addingham today. This one-span Burr truss design crossed Darby Creek and was built during the 1870s. The covered bridge was replaced in 1923. (Courtesy of Theodore Burr Covered Bridge Society of Pennsylvania.)

The Gradyville Road (John Thornton's) Covered Bridge, seen here in 1923, was constructed over Crum Creek between Edgemont and Newtown in Delaware County. This was a one-span Burr truss design that had a length of 56 feet. The covered bridge was demolished in 1925 to make room for a reservoir. (Courtesy of Theodore Burr Covered Bridge Society of Pennsylvania.)

The Northbrook (Marshall's Mill) Covered Bridge was constructed in 1807 over the West Branch of the Brandywine Creek in Chester County. This Burr truss covered bridge had a length of 98 feet. It existed until 1953 and was said to possibly have been the first covered bridge built in Chester County. (Courtesy of Theodore Burr Covered Bridge Society of Pennsylvania.)

Shaw's (Buffington Ford) Covered Bridge crossed the East Branch of the Brandywine Creek in West Bradford Township, Chester County. Nathan Y. Jester built the bridge in 1862 for $2,130. It got its name from Francis and William Shaw and William Buffington, who owned land at this site. The covered bridge was the victim of arson in 1953. (Courtesy of Walter W. Pryse.)

Pyle's Mill Twin Bridges were built in 1856 between Chester and Delaware Counties, two miles south of Chadd's Ford. One bridge crossed the Brandywine Creek, while the other served as a flood bridge. William Gamble and Nathan Y. Jester are credited with constructing the spans. They were removed in 1924. (Courtesy of Walter W. Pryse.)

The Steelville Covered Bridge was erected five miles southwest of Atglen between Chester and Lancaster Counties. In 1847, George Fink and George Hinkle constructed this Burr truss bridge over the East Branch of the Octoraro Creek at a cost of $800. The span existed until 1941, when a concrete bridge replaced it. This photograph was taken on December 8, 1938. (Courtesy of Walter W. Pryse.)

McCleary's Covered Bridge was constructed in 1889 over Black Run Creek in Nottingham Township in Chester County by George H. Jones at a cost of $2,116. There was a bridge of some sort built here prior to this incarnation. The 1889 covered bridge was the victim of arson on May 27, 1967. Herbert Richter took this photograph on November 23, 1958. (Courtesy of Herbert Richter.)

The Parkerford Covered Bridge crossed the Schuylkill River between Parkerford in Chester County and Linfield in Limerick Township, Montgomery County. The 1849 covered bridge was a three-span Town truss design with a length of 440 feet. The building on the right was the old tollhouse that charged usage fees until 1891. The covered bridge was replaced in 1932. (Courtesy of Walter W. Pryse.)

The Parkerford Covered Bridge took its name from the town of Parkerford in Chester County. The town got its name from a Parker's Ford, which was in existence before the covered bridge was built. Before bridges were constructed, the only way for people to cross a stream or river was to drive their wagon through the water or over the ice in the winter. In the spring, the water could become deep and dangerous due to heavy rain, and in the winter, the ice could be thin at spots and give way. Some larger crossings had ferries. It was at Parker's Ford that George Washington and his American Army forded the stream on September 19, 1777. Note the roofs over the windows to keep the rain out. Also, take note of the large stone piers supporting the covered bridge. (Courtesy of Theodore Burr Covered Bridge Society of Pennsylvania.)

This was the Haupt's Mill Covered Bridge over Cook's Creek near Durham in Springfield Township, Bucks County. The Town truss covered bridge, built in 1872, had a length of 107 feet. With a few exceptions, most of the covered bridges that were erected in Bucks County were Town truss designs. Arson was the cause of the fire that destroyed the bridge on January 14, 1985. (Courtesy of Theodore Burr Covered Bridge Society of Pennsylvania.)

The Finland Covered Bridge, seen here in April 1934, was constructed at Finland in Milford Township, Bucks County. The 1861 covered bridge was constructed using a Town lattice truss and crossed the Unami Creek. Note the many sideboards that are missing and the view of the Town truss under the sideboards. The covered bridge was demolished on May 1, 1938. (Courtesy of Walter W. Pryse.)

The Colmar (J. Becks) Covered Bridge was a borderline bridge built on County Line Road separating New Britain Township in Bucks County and Hatfield Township in Montgomery County. The 1828 covered bridge crossed the West Branch of the Neshaminy Creek near Line Lexington and was demolished in 1937. (Courtesy of Walter W. Pryse.)

The Castle Valley Covered Bridge crossed the Neshaminy Creek at the hamlet of Castle Valley in Bucks County. This three-span Town truss covered bridge, erected in 1835, had a length of 483 feet. Castle Valley got its name from Thomas "Crazy Tom" Meredith, who tried to erect a castle on a hill overlooking the valley. The covered bridge was demolished in 1930. (Author's collection.)

The Mill Creek (Rockville) Covered Bridge was over Mill Creek near Langhorn in Northampton Township, Bucks County. The Town truss covered design, built about 1830, was demolished in 1936. The bridge was near "Dripping Spring," a famous natural curiosity that dripped onto overhanging rocks. This photograph was taken in August 1936. (Author's collection.)

Krout's Mill Covered Bridge was constructed near Pipersville in Bedminister Township, Bucks County. The one-span Town truss covered bridge crossed over Deep Run and was known as bridge No. 177, a number given to the bridge by the county. Note the stepped portal and the rounded opening of the portal in this early photograph. The bridge was removed in 1938. (Author's collection.)

This is the Dead Waters (Upper) Covered Bridge over Crooked Creek near the village of Tioga in Tioga County. The Plank Road Company, which was a toll road company, erected the covered bridge in 1851. Plank (wooden) roads were in vogue during the 1840s and 1850s to eliminate muddy impassable roads. The one-span Burr truss bridge, about 120 feet in length, appears in bad shape in this photograph. The bridge was demolished in 1932. (Courtesy of Mazie S. Bodine.)

The Watrous Covered Bridge was built over the Pine Creek at the village of Watrous in Gaines Township, Tioga County. This 1854 Burr truss covered span was replaced in 1936. Note that the sides of the bridge only cover the lower half. (Courtesy of Theodore Burr Covered Bridge Society of Pennsylvania.)

Spangler's (Ebberly's Mill) Covered Bridge was erected in 1850 over the Yellow Breeches Creek between Cumberland and York Counties. This one-span Burr truss covered bridge had a length of 134 feet measured from abutment to abutment or 150 feet measured from portal to portal. It was destroyed by fire on April 13, 1963. (Courtesy of Sara Boyle.)

Eyster's (Oyster's Mill/Heck's) Covered Bridge, also over the Conodoguinet Creek, was located northeast of Wormleysburg in East Pennsboro Township, Cumberland County. *Conodoguinet* is a Native American word meaning "a long way with many bends." This creek is 90 miles in length. Samuel Myers built the three-span Burr truss structure in 1881 at a cost of $5,410. On March 17, 1958, the 408-foot-long covered bridge burned down. (Courtesy of George R. Wills.)

Quigley's Twin Covered Bridges were built over the Conodoguinet Creek east of Newburg in Hopewell Township, Cumberland County. Jacob Bishop erected both Burr truss designs in 1824 at a cost of $5,350, but Quigley's No. 1 Bridge was an open span, whereas Quigley's No. 2 Bridge was a covered one. In 1834, Joseph Smith renovated Quigley's No. 1 Bridge as a covered bridge, and in 1860, John Gutshall reconstructed Quigley's No. 1 Bridge after it was badly damaged. Quigley's No. 2 Bridge was rebuilt in 1856 after being washed out in a flood. The photograph here shows the 1860 Quigley's No. 1 Bridge and the 1856 Quigley's No. 2 Bridge. On October 23, 1934, a coal truck tried to cross the twins and fell through the floor of the north twin. The floor was repaired, and the bridge was reopened to traffic the same year. The twins were replaced in 1947 with steel spans. (Courtesy of C.H. Thomas.)

The Newburg (Cats Cabin/Kats Cabin) Covered Bridge was located south of Newburg in Hopewell Township, Cumberland County. This Conodoguinet Creek crossing was constructed in 1834 by William LeBarron and James Wilson for $2,200 and replaced in 1933. A delivery wagon from the town of Newburg is seen on the covered bridge in this 1907 photograph. (Author's collection.)

The Mausteller Covered Bridge crossed Little Fishing Creek northeast of Buckhorn between Hemlock and Mount Pleasant Townships in Columbia County. A sign on the bridge in the photograph states, "Bridge Damaged, Wt. Limit 2 Ton." This one-span Burr truss design was erected in 1860 and was destroyed by a tropical storm on June 22, 1972. (Courtesy of Theodore Burr Covered Bridge Society of Pennsylvania.)

The Y Covered Bridge was built near the village of Central in Sugar Loaf Township, Columbia County. This one-span queen post trust design crossed the East Branch of Fishing Creek. J.M. Larish constructed the bridge in 1887 at a cost of $602.22. The bridge got its name from its location near the "Y" turnaround of the Bloomsburg and Sullivan Railroad. On August 15, 1983, it became the victim of arson. (Courtesy of Theodore Burr Covered Bridge Society of Pennsylvania.)

The Mordansville Covered Bridge was found in the village of Mordansville between Hemlock and Mount Pleasant Townships in Columbia County. This one-span Burr truss bridge crossed Little Fishing Creek until it was removed in 1963. (Courtesy of Theodore Burr Covered Bridge Society of Pennsylvania.)

The Joe Ash Covered Bridge was built in Benton Township in Columbia County. This covered bridge was a one-span queen post truss design that carried Route 663 over the Raven Creek. The bridge had a length of only 27 feet and was replaced in 1963. (Courtesy of Theodore Burr Covered Bridge Society of Pennsylvania.)

The Mill Grove Covered Bridge was erected at the village of Mill Grove in Roaring Creek Township, Columbia County. The one-span queen post truss bridge carried Mill Grove Road across Roaring Creek. It was replaced in 1956. (Courtesy of Theodore Burr Covered Bridge Society of Pennsylvania.)

The Hunter Station Covered Bridge reached over Mahanoy Creek on Creek Road in Little Mahanoy Township, Northumberland County. Peter Keefer built this one-span Burr truss bridge in 1869 for $1,345.55. It was washed away by a tropical storm on June 22, 1972. (Courtesy of Theodore Burr Covered Bridge Society of Pennsylvania.)

The Dewalt Covered Bridge crossed Delaware Run on River Road north of the village of Dewalt in Delaware Township, Northumberland County. Samuel L. Culp constructed this one-span multi-king post truss bridge in 1882. It was also washed away by a tropical storm on June 22, 1972. (Courtesy of Theodore Burr Covered Bridge Society of Pennsylvania.)

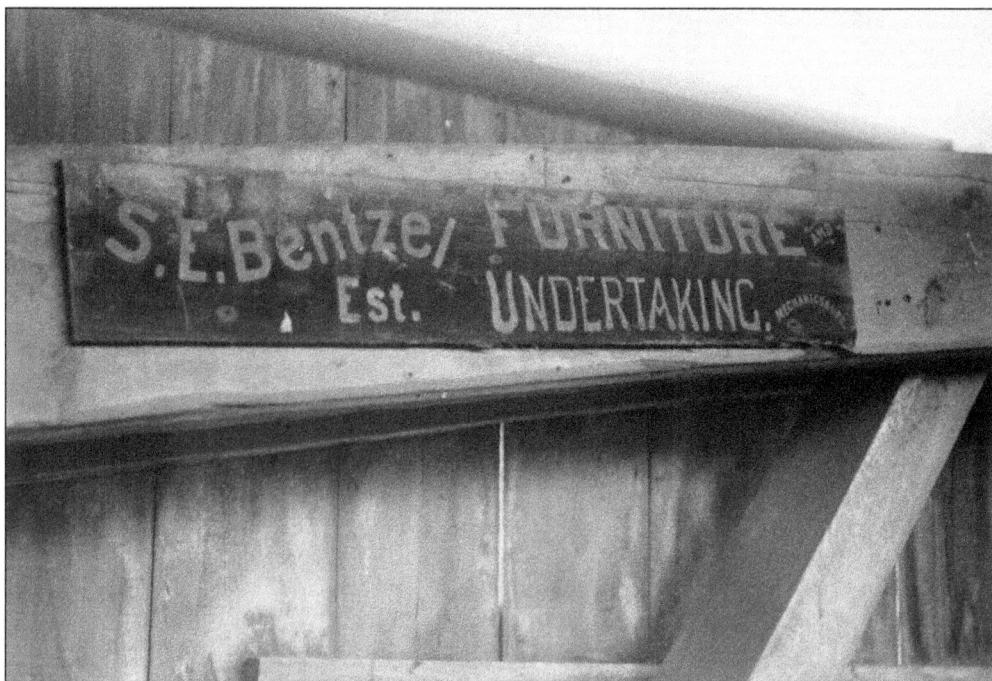

In the early years, it was common to see advertising on covered bridges as one approached a town. Here, S.E. Bentzel advertises his furniture and undertaking business near the town of Mechanicsburg in Cumberland County. (Courtesy of Theodore Burr Covered Bridge Society of Pennsylvania.)

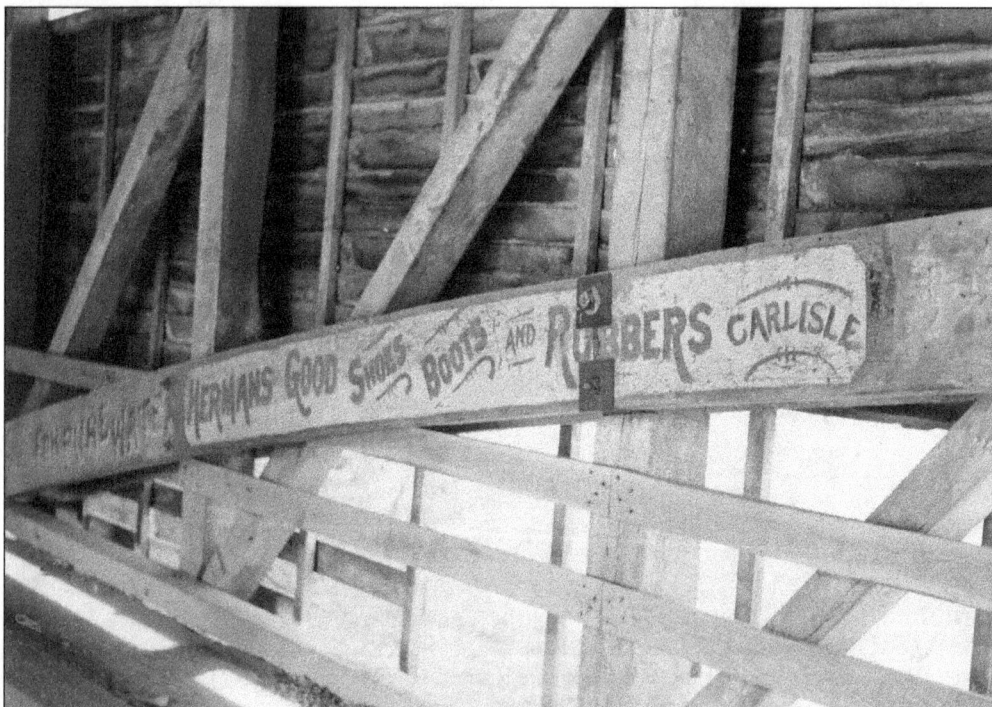

Here is an advertisement for Mermans Store for shoes, boots, and rubbers in the town of Carlisle in Cumberland County. (Courtesy of Theodore Burr Covered Bridge Society of Pennsylvania.)

The Sand Beach (Church Ford) Covered Bridge was built between Derry and South Hanover Townships north of Hershey in Dauphin County. This Swatara Creek crossing, constructed about 1853, was a two-span Burr truss bridge. (Courtesy of Theodore Burr Covered Bridge Society of Pennsylvania.)

The Sand Beach Covered Bridge was slated to be removed in 1961 and 1962, but local citizens prevented it by having the bridge bypassed. It was their hope it could be restored; however, on September 3, 1966, the 220-foot-long bridge was destroyed by arson and was never restored. (Courtesy of Theodore Burr Covered Bridge Society of Pennsylvania.)

This is the Clifton Covered Bridge with its reflection in the Swatara Creek in Dauphin County. It was situated northeast of Middletown between Derry and Lower Swatara Townships. The Clifton bridge was destroyed by floodwaters of a tropical storm on June 22, 1972. (Author's collection.)

The Cooper Farm Covered Bridge, seen here in May 1960, crossed the Wiconisco Creek west of Elizabethville in Washington Township, Dauphin County. This one-span Burr truss crossing was also lost during the tropical storm on June 22, 1972. (Courtesy of Theodore Burr Covered Bridge Society of Pennsylvania.)

44

Fiddler's Elbow Covered Bridge connected Derry and Lower Swatara Townships southwest of Hummelstown in Dauphin County. This two-span Burr truss covered bridge, built in 1862, crossed the Swatara Creek. Fiddler's Elbow got its name from a sharp bend in the river at this location. The bridge was washed out in a flood on June 22, 1972. (Author's collection.)

Price's (Weimer) Covered Bridge, seen here in June 1958, crossed Brush Creek in West Providence Township, Bedford County. The one-span Burr truss crossing was built on Pointer Road in 1902 and had a length of 126 feet. At one time, Bedford County had over 60 covered bridges; today, only 14 covered bridges remain. The covered bridge was replaced in 1961. (Courtesy of Theodore Burr Covered Bridge Society of Pennsylvania.)

The Mainville Covered Bridge was located south of the village of Mainville over the Catawissa Creek in Columbia County. This one-span Burr truss bridge's date of construction is unknown. Hurricane Agnes destroyed the Mainville Bridge on June 22, 1972. (Courtesy of Theodore Burr Covered Bridge Society of Pennsylvania.)

Copyright 1903 by the Rotograph Co.

A 5892 Ferry and the remains of the Susquehanna Bridge, Danville, Pa.

Be sure to come up Saturday A. M. at the latest. Verna.

The Danville (Riverside) Covered Bridge crossed the North Branch of the Susquehanna River at Danville in Montour County. This 1829 was a seven-span Burr truss bridge with a length of 1,350 feet. On March 17, 1875, it collapsed and was rebuilt as a Howe truss bridge. A flood destroyed this second covered span, pictured here, on March 9, 1904. Note the ferry in the foreground that was put back into use. (Author's collection.)

The Lock Haven-Lockport Covered Bridge was built over the West Branch of the Susquehanna River at Lock Haven in Clinton County. This four-span Burr truss bridge was erected in 1852 at a cost of $25,000 and had a length of 840 feet. A pedestrian walkway that was shared with mules of the Susquehanna Canal towpath is visible. The building on the left was the tollhouse. (Courtesy of Thomas E. Walczak.)

The local church named the town Lock Haven because it had a canal lock and became a haven for loggers, boatmen, and other travelers. This photograph of the Lock Haven–Lockport Covered Bridge was taken from the north bank in Lockport looking toward Lock Haven. It was destroyed by fire on June 27, 1919. (Author's collection.)

The Blue Hill (Red) Covered Bridge crossed the West Branch of the Susquehanna River at Northumberland. It was built in 1828 by Reuben Field and was part of the Pennsylvania Canal System. This Burr truss covered bridge had five spans, was 1,300 feet in length, and connected the town of Northumberland to Union County. (Courtesy of Theodore Burr Covered Bridge Society of Pennsylvania.)

The Old Lock and Bridge over Susquehanna River, Northumberland, Pa.

The Blue Hill Covered Bridge had two travel lanes and two pedestrian walkways. Pedestrians and canal mules shared the walkways. A flood in June 1889 washed out the center spans, but they were rebuilt later that year. On June 30, 1923, the bridge was destroyed by fire. (Courtesy of Thomas E. Walczak.)

48

Clark's Ferry Covered Bridge stretched over the Susquehanna River above Harrisburg at Duncannon. This Dauphin County Burr truss covered design was built in 1836. There was a prior Town truss covered bridge at this location, built between 1828 and 1829, but the first covered bridge had to be replaced because of serious defects. (Courtesy of Vera H. Wagner.)

CLARKS FERRY BRIDGE, DUNCANNON, PA.

In 1846, fire from a steam-powered tugboat making repairs to the Clark's Ferry Bridge destroyed the bridge; it was rebuilt in 1847. In 1850, arson was the cause of the bridge being destroyed again, and it was once again reconstructed. Finally, in March 1946, a flood destroyed the covered bridge. This photograph was taken on December 24, 1925. (Courtesy of Theodore Burr Covered Bridge Society of Pennsylvania.)

The Camelback Covered Bridge crossed the Susquehanna River at Harrisburg. Theodore Burr built the 11-span Burr truss bridge from 1812 to 1817; it was actually two separate bridges resting on an island. The first bridge shown here went from Lemoyne (Cumberland County) on the west shore to City Island (Dauphin County) in the middle of the Susquehanna River. It was this western span that had a hump-like appearance due to higher piers, lending the name "Camelback." This bridge was replaced in 1903. (Courtesy of Theodore Burr Covered Bridge Society of Pennsylvania.)

The second span of the Camelback Covered Bridge went from City Island to Harrisburg. This eastern span had more of a level appearance. In 1902, there was a flood that caused serious damage to the bridge, and it had to be replaced with a more modern structure. (Courtesy of Jim Smedley.)

This is another photograph of the Camelback Covered Bridge taken from the western shore looking toward Harrisburg. It took Theodore Burr five years to build this crossing, partly because he was building three other covered bridges across the Susquehanna River at the same time. (Courtesy of Theodore Burr Covered Bridge Society of Pennsylvania.)

This is an interior view of the Camelback Covered Bridge. Note the rise of the floor in the humpback-like bridge and the ladder in the lower right of the photograph. The average toll for each score of cattle was 25¢; the toll for each score of sheep or hogs was 12.5¢. (Courtesy of Theodore Burr Covered Bridge Society of Pennsylvania.)

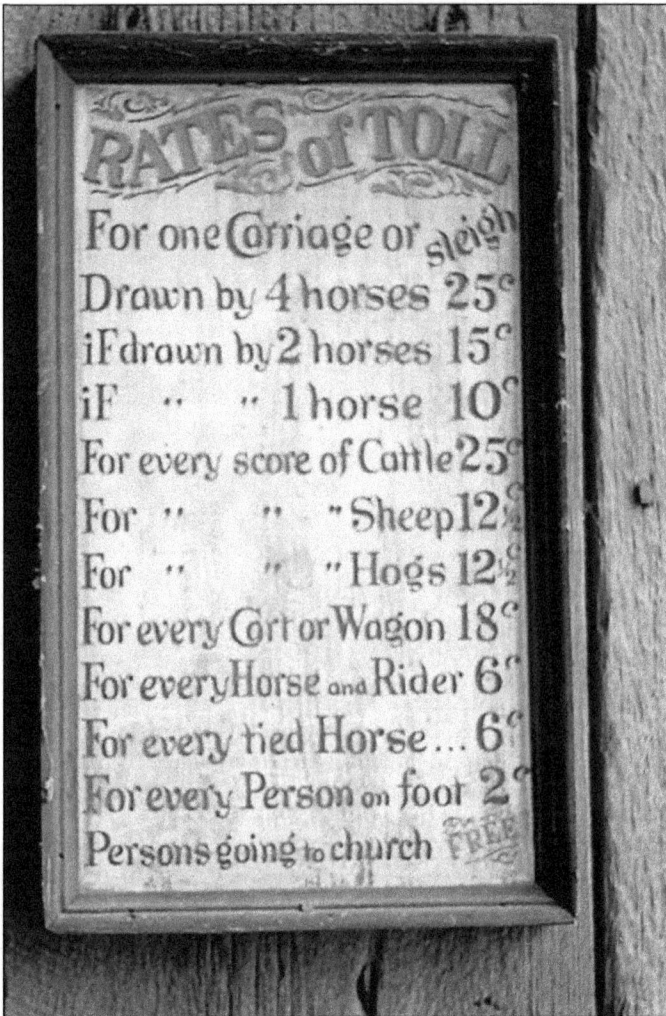

These were the tolls charged to cross the long Clark's Ferry Covered Bridge over the Susquehanna River at Harrisburg. The river is almost a mile wide at the point this tollbooth was located. The tolls charged to cross normal-sized covered bridges were less. (Author's collection.)

RATES of TOLL

For one Carriage or sleigh
Drawn by 4 horses 25ᶜ
iF drawn by 2 horses 15ᶜ
iF "   " 1 horse 10ᶜ
For every score of Cattle 25ᶜ
For "   " " Sheep 12½ᶜ
For "   " " Hogs 12½ᶜ
For every Cart or Wagon 18ᶜ
For every Horse and Rider 6ᶜ
For every tied Horse... 6ᶜ
For every Person on foot 2ᶜ
Persons going to church FREE

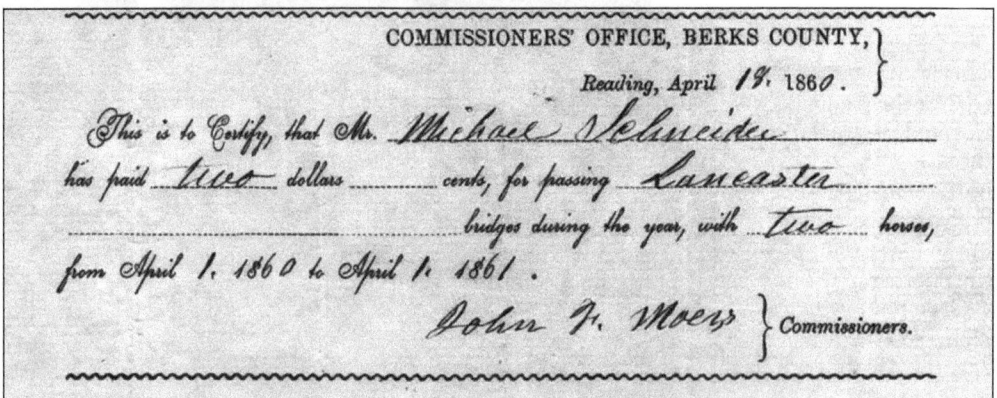

COMMISSIONERS' OFFICE, BERKS COUNTY,
Reading, April 1ˢᵗ 1860.

This is to Certify, that Mr. _Michael Schneider_ has paid _two_ dollars _____ cents, for passing _Lancaster_ bridges during the year, with _two_ horses, from April 1. 1860 to April 1. 1861.

John F. Moers } Commissioners.

This is a receipt for a toll bridge fee at Reading in 1860. For $2, this man could cross the bridge whenever he wanted for a whole year with a wagon and two horses. If one crossed it frequently, it was much cheaper to prepay the tolls for the year rather than pay tolls each time the bridge was crossed. (Author's collection.)

The Jollytown Covered Bridge crossed Dunkard Creek in Gilmore Township, Greene County. Jollytown was named after its founder, Titus Jolly. The 1882 queen post truss covered bridge had a length of 44 feet and was replaced in 1961. This photograph was taken on June 4, 1960, by John E. Humphreys. (Courtesy of Thomas E. Walczak.)

The Hero Bridge stretched across the Pennsylvania Fork of Dunkard Creek southwest of the Jollytown in Gilmore Township, Greene County. The bridge was located a quarter mile north of the Mason Dixon Line, which separated Pennsylvania and West Virginia. L.M. Hennen built this one-span queen post crossing in 1887. The bridge collapsed in 1977. This photograph was taken on June 4, 1960, by John E. Humphreys. (Courtesy of Thomas E. Walczak.)

This is McConnell's Mills Covered Bridge, which was once situated between the villages of Burgertsville and Westland in Chartiers Township, Washington County. This one-span queen post truss bridge crossed Chartiers Run and had a length of 49 feet. The photograph was taken on June 22, 1947. The covered bridge was replaced in 1951. (Author's collection.)

The J. McDonald's (Caldwell) Covered Bridge was on Old Brick Road over Wheeling Creek between Donegal and West Finley Townships in Washington County. A close look at the photograph shows the brick road. This one-span king post truss bridge was replaced in 1955. (Author's collection.)

East End Bridge, Brownsville, Pa.

The Brownsville Covered Bridge was built in 1833 over the Monongahela River between Brownsville, Fayette County, and West Brownsville, Washington County. Brownsville was at one time an industrial center and transportation hub. The covered bridge had two roadway lanes and a pedestrian walkway lane. Note how close the railroad tracks are from the entrance to the bridge. It was replaced in 1911. (Author's collection.)

The Forty-third Street Bridge crossed the Allegheny River in the Lawrenceville section of Pittsburgh. The four-span Burr truss covered bridge was built in 1870, was over 900 feet in length, and had a pedestrian sidewalk. The signage on the portal states, "Drive No Faster Than A Walk Penalty $5.00." When replaced in 1924, it was the last standing covered bridge in Pittsburgh. (Courtesy of Theodore Burr Covered Bridge Society of Pennsylvania.)

This is an early-1930s photograph of the Bunker Hill Covered Bridge in Lebanon County. Note the floodwaters flowing through the covered bridge and the man walking out. The flood did not seriously damage the structure. (Courtesy of Theodore Burr Covered Bridge Society of Pennsylvania.)

These two covered bridges were called Harper's Tavern Twin Bridges, located at Harper's Tavern in East Hanover Township, Lebanon County. On the left is Harper's Tavern Twin No. 1 Bridge. This two-span crossing, built in 1863, stretched over the Swatara Creek. On the right is Harper's Tavern Twin No. 2 Bridge. This one-span Burr truss design carried Route 22 over Indiantown Creek. Both bridges were replaced in 1904. (Courtesy of George R. Wills.)

The Bunker Hill Covered Bridge was located a quarter mile south of Jonestown in Lebanon County. This was Lebanon County's last remaining covered bridge. This two-span Burr truss design crossed the Little Swatara Creek and had a length of 226 feet. (Author's collection.)

The Westmount Station Covered Bridge was built in North Lebanon Township at Westmount Station, Lebanon County. The one-span, yellow-colored crossing was built by the railroad to carry traffic over the tracks of the Lebanon and Freemont branch of the Reading Railroad. A man once hung himself from the bottom of the bridge. It was destroyed by fire in 1939. (Courtesy of George R. Wills.)

The McDaniel's Covered Bridge carried Trail 419 (Bennett Road) across Brush Creek midway between Everett and Breezewood in Bedford County. Jacob Fries built this one-span multi-king post truss crossing in 1873. The 118-foot-long covered bridge connected East Providence and West Providence Townships. (Courtesy of Theodore Burr Covered Bridge Society of Pennsylvania.)

These are the remains of the McDaniel's Covered Bridge after vandals deliberately set it on fire on Easter Sunday, April 3, 1988; nothing was salvageable. This was one of 36 covered bridges erected in Bedford County. (Courtesy of Theodore Burr Covered Bridge Society of Pennsylvania.)

The Yount Station Covered Bridge was constructed in 1875 over Dunnings Creek in Bedford County. This one-span Burr truss bridge was north of Bedford near the town of Mench. The bridge was replaced in 1961. (Courtesy of Theodore Burr Covered Bridge Society of Pennsylvania.)

Hughes Covered Bridge also crossed Dunnings Creek and was located near Bedford in Bedford County. This one-span Burr truss design had a length of 96 feet. It was built in 1878 by J.H. Thompson and stood until it was replaced in 1961. (Courtesy of Theodore Burr Covered Bridge Society of Pennsylvania.)

Beck's Mill Covered Bridge crossed Bixler's Run in northeast Madison Township, Perry County. Ward Mulligan and F.J. Adair erected the one-span Burr truss bridge in 1916. It was removed in 1950. This photograph was taken in November 1949. (Courtesy of Theodore Burr Covered Bridge Society of Pennsylvania.)

Perry County's Bridgeport Covered Bridge stretched across Sherman's Creek in Spring Township at the town of Bridgeport. The two-span Burr truss covered bridge was built in 1868 and was removed in 1954. There were over 40 covered bridges constructed in Perry County. Today, only 14 covered bridges remain. (Courtesy of Theodore Burr Covered Bridge Society of Pennsylvania.)

Bryansville Covered Bridge was located three-fourths of a mile northeast of Bryansville in Peach Bottom Township, York County. This one-span Burr truss bridge had a length of 63 feet and crossed Scott Creek. This photograph is believed to have been taken in 1950 during the demolition of the bridge. (Courtesy of Theodore Burr Covered Bridge Society of Pennsylvania.)

Eisenhart's Mill (Big Eisenhart's Mill) Covered Bridge, seen here in 1951, was built around 1862 between Washington and Paradise Township in York County. This one-span Burr truss design had a length of 197 feet and crossed the Conewago Creek. The covered bridge was replaced in 1958. (Courtesy of George R. Wills.)

Kohler's Mill Covered Bridge was built over Swift Run between Mount Pleasant and Straban Townships in Adams County. This was a one-span Burr truss bridge with fancy cut-stepped portals. There had been 49 covered bridges in Adams County, but today, only 4 remain. (Author's collection.)

Brown's Mill Covered Bridge was situated three miles west of East Berlin Borough between Hamilton and Reading Townships in Adams County. This one-span Howe truss covered bridge crossed the Conewago Creek and was removed in 1958. (Courtesy of Theodore Burr Covered Bridge Society of Pennsylvania.)

Kuhn's Fording Covered Bridge was located northwest of Adamstown at East Berlin in Adams County. The two-span Burr truss bridge was erected in 1862 and had a length of 228 feet measured portal to portal. (Courtesy of Theodore Burr Covered Bridge Society of Pennsylvania.)

Kuhn's Fording Bridge crossed the Conewago Creek and was destroyed by Hurricane Eloise on September 9, 1975. It was dismantled and given to Lancaster County to be used for spare parts to repair bridges in Lancaster County. (Courtesy of Theodore Burr Covered Bridge Society of Pennsylvania.)

The Port Clinton Covered Bridge was built in 1866 over the Little Schuylkill River at Port Clinton in Schuylkill County. During the 1800s, large shipments of coal were brought to Port Clinton on railroad cars and loaded onto the barges of the Schuylkill Canal Company for transport to towns to the south. Port Clinton was once an important center of trade and transportation. Trains are visible in the background of the photograph. (Author's collection.)

The Schuylkill Haven Covered Bridge was constructed on Columbia Street in Schuylkill Haven, Schuylkill County. John Hughes first built this bridge in 1829 for $1,480, and after it was destroyed by a flood, it was rebuilt in 1851 at a cost of $2,400 as pictured here. This one-span Burr truss design crossed the Schuylkill River and was in existence until 1922, when it was replaced. (Author's collection.)

The Taylorsville's (Bickel's/ Reed's) Mill Covered Bridge was located near Taylorsville in Barry Township, Schuylkill County. This two-span Burr truss covered bridge had a length of 156 feet and crossed the Mahanoy Creek. The bridge was destroyed by the high winds of a hurricane in 1955. Note its two distinctive sets of Burr arches. (Courtesy of Schuylkill County Courthouse.)

The Stanhope Covered Bridge was situated a half mile northeast of Stanhope on the road to Pine Grove in Pine Grove Township, Schuylkill County. This was a short 64-foot-long Burr truss design that crossed Lower Little Swatara Creek. The covered bridge was gone before 1946. Barely visible in this side-view photograph is the fancy stepped portal design on the ends of the bridge. (Courtesy of the Schuylkill County Courthouse.)

The Port Royal Covered Bridge carried Market Street across the Juniata River between the town of Port Royal and Walker Township in Juniata County. The four-span Burr truss crossing was built in 1892 at a cost of $16,500. There had been earlier covered bridges at this location. This structure, also known locally as the "River Bridge," was destroyed by floodwaters on March 18, 1936. (Courtesy of Theodore Burr Covered Bridge Society of Pennsylvania.)

This 1818 two-span, two-lane covered bridge carried Route 30 (Lincoln Highway) over the Raystown Branch of the Juniata River in Bedford County. In 1889, a flood washed away one span of the bridge, and a new one was built but with only one lane. When traveling through the one-lane span, travelers would approach a dangerous partition of the two-lane span. A flood destroyed the bridge in 1936. (Courtesy of Vera H. Wagner.)

In 1815, William LeBaron built this three-span covered toll bridge at the southern end of Beaver Falls in Beaver County at a cost of $15,000. This two-lane bridge was 500 feet in length and crossed Beaver River. A sign seen on the portal forbids people from carrying an open flame on the bridge or crossing faster than a walk; the fine for such an offense was $5. (Author's collection.)

This was the West Newton Covered Bridge over the Youghiogheny River in Westmoreland County. This double-lane, three-span design was constructed in 1833 and had a length of 482 feet. There was a pedestrian sidewalk on the downstream side of it. The covered bridge was replaced in 1907. (Author's collection.)

The Troutman Covered Bridge crossed the Mahantango Creek between Dauphin and Northumberland Counties. This one-span Burr truss crossing was erected in 1839 near the village of Hebe. E.D. Messner rebuilt the bridge, No. 86, in 1890. Troutman's Bridge was destroyed by Hurricane Agnes on June 22, 1972. (Courtesy of Theodore Burr Covered Bridge Society of Pennsylvania.)

The Riegel Covered Bridge crossed Roaring Creek in Franklin Township, Columbia County. This one-span Burr truss design was built in 1871 by Jacob Kostenbauder at a cost of $1,882.50. This bridge, No. 6, was the victim of arson on May 30, 1979. (Courtesy of Theodore Burr Covered Bridge Society of Pennsylvania.)

The Portland-Columbia Covered Bridge was built over the Delaware River between Portland, Northampton County, Pennsylvania, and Columbia, Warren County, New Jersey. This 1869 four-span Burr truss crossing was over 700 feet in length. It was originally a toll bridge until it was bought by the county and made toll-free in 1927. The last toll collector at the bridge was Charles J. Baker. (Courtesy of Theodore Burr Covered Bridge Society of Pennsylvania.)

In its later years, the covered bridge (seen here in 1951) became known as the "Coke Bridge." An advertisement was painted on the entire side of it stating "5¢ sold everywhere 5¢ Coca-Cola." This was far larger than any billboard seen today. A flood destroyed the covered bridge in 1955. (Courtesy of Theodore Burr Covered Bridge Society of Pennsylvania.)

The Easton-Phillipsburg Covered Bridge, built by Timothy Palmer at a cost of $90,000, was opened to traffic on October 14, 1806. Prior to the bridge, ferry service at this location began in 1739. The three-span, 550-foot-long design crossed the Delaware River and connected Easton, Pennsylvania, to Phillipsburg (Northampton Street), New Jersey. Note the house-like windows adorning the bridge. This photograph was taken during high water. (Courtesy of Walter W. Pryse.)

A notice on the portal of the Easton-Phillipsburg Covered Bridge states, "CAUTION, Keep to the right, All persons keep to the right and walk only." Note the tracks going into the bridge, which were first used for horse-drawn streetcars and later by trolley cars. The covered bridge was replaced in 1895. (Courtesy of Theodore Burr Covered Bridge Society of Pennsylvania.)

THE BRIDGE, Milford, N. J.

The Upper Black Eddy-Milford Covered Bridge was constructed over the Delaware River between Upper Black Eddy, Bucks County, Pennsylvania, and Milford, Hunterdon County, New Jersey. The 1862 three-span Burr truss crossing had a length of 666 feet. There was an earlier covered bridge, built here in 1842, that was destroyed by a flood. (Author's collection.)

This is the interior of the Upper Black Eddy-Milford Covered Bridge. Note the double set of massive arches. Some of the tolls for this bridge included 3¢ to cross one way with a bicycle and 25¢ to cross one way for circus teams. This span was replaced by a steel truss bridge in 1933. (Courtesy of Theodore Burr Covered Bridge Society of Pennsylvania.)

The Uhlerstown-Frenchtown (Alexandria) Covered Bridge was built over the Delaware River between Bucks County, Pennsylvania, and Hunterdon County, New Jersey. This six-span Burr truss design was constructed in 1862 for $20,000. It replaced an earlier bridge that had been erected in 1844. In this photograph, two covered spans on the New Jersey side were destroyed by a flood on October 10, 1903, and replaced by two steel truss spans. The entire structure became a steel truss bridge in 1931. (Author's collection.)

The Point Pleasant Covered Bridge was a five-span Delaware River crossing that connected Point Pleasant in Bucks County, Pennsylvania, and Byram in Hunterdon County, New Jersey. The covered bridge, built in 1862, was 895 feet in length. It was destroyed by fire on March 29, 1892. (Courtesy of Walter W. Pryse.)

The Lumberville Covered Bridge was constructed over the Delaware River and Delaware Canal between Lumberville, Bucks County, Pennsylvania, and Raven Rock, Hunterdon County, New Jersey. The five-span Town truss bridge had a length of 705 feet. One span stretched over the canal, and four spans crossed the river. Solon Chapin and Anthony Fry built the covered toll bridge in 1835. (Courtesy of Walter W. Pryse.)

On October 10, 1903, one span of the Lumberville Covered Bridge was washed out during high waters. It was replaced with an iron span, shown in this image. Some examples of tolls for this bridge included 2¢ for pedestrians, 1¢ for wheelbarrows, and 5¢ per horse for carriages. The bridge stood until it was removed in 1947. (Author's collection.)

The Centre-Stockton Covered Bridge connected Centre Bridge, Bucks County, Pennsylvania, to Stockton, Hunterdon County, New Jersey. Courtland Yardley built this six-span design in 1841 at a cost of $42,000. There had been two previous covered bridges at this location over the Delaware River. (Courtesy of Theodore Burr Covered Bridge Society of Pennsylvania.)

This view of the Centre-Stockton Covered Bridge is from the New Jersey side of the Delaware River. The tollhouse is on the right, and the first toll collector was Joel Abel. On June 6, 1862, three spans of the covered bridge were washed away by a flood and eventually replaced by three new covered spans. (Courtesy of Theodore Burr Covered Bridge Society of Pennsylvania.)

In this photograph of the Centre-Stockton Bridge, take note of the high piers meant to keep the bridge safe from the high floodwaters of the Delaware River. On at least one occasion, as mentioned on the previous page, these piers were not high enough. On July 22, 1923, the bridge was hit by lightning and destroyed by fire. (Author's collection.)

The 1814 New Hope Covered Bridge crossed the Delaware River from New Hope, Pennsylvania to Lambertville, New Jersey. A sign over the portal reads, "Five dollar fine over and above the damages for driving or riding faster than a walk over this bridge, or for taking more than ten horses or cattle in one drove, or for smoking or carrying a cigar or pipe." The bridge was destroyed by a flood on October 10, 1903. (Author's collection.)

The Upper Trenton (Calhoun Street) Covered Bridge crossed the Delaware River between Trenton, New Jersey, and Morrisville in Bucks County, Pennsylvania. This seven-span Burr truss crossing was built by the Trenton City Bridge Company in 1861 for $60,000. The covered bridge, which was 1,274 feet in length and consisted of two roadway lanes and two pedestrian walkways, was destroyed by fire on June 25, 1884. (Courtesy of Theodore Burr Covered Bridge Society of Pennsylvania.)

This photograph of a Burr truss multi-span covered bridge is simply labeled, "Bridge over Delaware River." Think of all the lumber and hard work that went into building large covered bridges such as this one. (Courtesy Theodore Burr Covered Bridge Society of Pennsylvania.)

Two

PENNSYLVANIA'S PRESENT COVERED BRIDGES

This is the Pleasantville Covered Bridge in Berks County. It was built in 1852 as an uncovered bridge. In 1856, the sides were raised, and a roof was installed. Today, visitors can see the top chord of the 1852 uncovered bridge about three feet above the floor. This photograph was taken in the 1940s when the bridge was painted white. (Courtesy of Richard T. Donovan.)

Griesemer's Mill Covered Bridge is located north of Spangsville in Oley Township, Berks County. The bridge crosses the Manatawny Creek and was named for the mill standing next it. This 1868 one-span Burr truss design has crosswise floorboards that rattle when cars travel through it. The photograph was taken when the bridge still had a fancy portal. (Author's collection.)

The Dreibelbis Station Covered Bridge is situated between Virginville and Lenhartsville just off of Route 143 in Berks County. Charles Kutz and Simon Dreibelbis built the one-span Burr truss crossing over Maiden Creek in 1869. In this early photograph, note the building on the right that was once an icehouse. Ice was harvested from the creek in the winter and stored here to be used in the summer to keep food cold. (Courtesy of Walter W. Pryse.)

Kutz's Mill Covered Bridge is on Route 798 (Kutz Mill Road), approximately two miles north of Kutztown. This 1854 one-span Burr truss bridge crosses the Sacony Creek and is Berks County's shortest covered bridge at 90 feet in length. The crossing is unusual in that it has a concrete floor that was installed in 1958. Kutz's Mill stands next to the bridge. (Author's collection.)

Wertz's Mill (Red) Covered Bridge, seen here in the 1930s, is located in the Heritage Center off of Route 222 north of Reading. Amandas Knerr built it in 1867 at a cost of $7,450. Wertz's Bridge is the longest single-span covered bridge in Pennsylvania. It is also home to a colony of over 200 little brown bats. (Courtesy of Walter W. Pryse.)

The Banks Covered Bridge is located on Route 476 in Willington Township, Lawrence County. This one-span Burr truss design was constructed in 1889 over the Neshannock Creek. Both the inside and the outside of the bridge are painted white. (Courtesy of Heather and Ulles Fox.)

McConnell's Mill and McConnell's Mill Covered Bridge can both be seen in this photograph. The bridge is on Route 415, McConnell's Mill Road, in McConnell's Mill State Park. The 1874 one-span Howe truss design crosses Slippery Rock Creek in a beautiful park setting. This Lawrence County covered bridge is one of only five Howe truss covered bridges left in Pennsylvania. (Courtesy of Heather and Ulles Fox.)

The Forksville Covered Bridge crosses the Loyalsock Creek on Bridge Street in Forksville, Sullivan County. The bridge is located just off of Route 154 north of Worlds End State Park. It was erected in 1850 by Sadler Rogers and has a 15-foot width. (Photograph by Timothy J. Moll.)

The Forksville Covered Bridge is a one-span Burr truss design with a length of 163 feet. The bridge is used frequently because the Forksville General Store is on one side and the main highway is on the other. Today, this is the only general store and restaurant for miles around. (Photograph by Timothy J. Moll.)

Burkholder's (Beechdale/Althouse's) Covered Bridge is located 2.2 miles northeast of the town of Garrett on Trail 548 in Somerset County. The 1870 one-span covered bridge crosses Buffalo Creek in Brothers Valley Township. (Photograph by Andrew J. Moll.)

Only the lower half of Burkholder's Covered Bridge has siding. While this allows plenty of light to enter the bridge, it also allows rain to enter. Also, note how low the Burr arch is compared to most other bridges where the arch comes quite close to the roof. (Photograph by Andrew J. Moll.)

The Glessner Covered Bridge is located four-fifths of a mile north of the village of Shanksville on Route 565 in Stony Creek Township, Somerset County. This 1881 one-span Burr truss design crosses Stony Creek. Most of the covered bridges of Somerset County have the name over the portal. (Photograph by Andrew J. Moll.)

The Colvin Covered Bridge is located one mile southwest of the town of Schellsburg in Napier Township, Bedford County. This 1880 one-span multi-king post truss covered bridge takes Route 443 across Shawnee Creek. There is siding on only its lower third. Most covered bridges in Bedford and Somerset Counties have a narrow width, more so than other county bridges. (Photograph by Andrew J. Moll.)

Geiger's Covered Bridge is on Route 681, about 2.5 miles northwest of Kernsville, in Lehigh County. This one-span Burr truss crossing was built in 1860 over Jordan Creek. Note the water pipe on the left, which was used to pump water from the creek through the bridge to local farms and an orchard. (Author's collection.)

Manasses Guth Covered Bridge carries Route 602 over Jordan Creek near Orefield in South Whitehall Township, Lehigh County. The crossing was named after Manasses Guth, who owned farmland next it. Constructed in 1868, this is a one-span Burr truss bridge. (Author's collection.)

Bogert's Covered Bridge is located in Lehigh County, south of Allentown, in Little Lehigh Park. The 1841 one-span Burr truss bridge is located in a scenic part of the Lehigh Valley and provides great photographic opportunities. In this old image, the bridge is painted white; however, it is painted red today. (Author's collection.)

Rex's Covered Bridge is situated on Route 593, one mile northwest of Kernsville, in Lehigh County. This 1858 one-span Burr truss design crosses Jordan Creek. One unusual feature of this bridge is a stop sign located in its interior. (Author's collection.)

The Academia (Pomeroy Mill) Covered Bridge is located west of Port Royal between Beale and Spruce Hill Townships in Juniata County. James M. Groninger built this two-span Burr truss bridge over the Tuscarora Creek in 1902. With a length of 278 feet, it is considered the longest currently standing covered bridge in the state. This photograph was taken on October 11, 1959. (Courtesy of Walter W. Pryse.)

The Davis Covered Bridge stands northwest of Slabtown in Cleveland Township, Columbia County. This is a one-span Burr truss design that crosses the North Branch of Roaring Creek. Daniel Kostenbauder constructed the bridge in 1875 at a cost of $1,248.88. In this photograph, the bridge is decorated with corn shocks for the fall season of 1985. (Author's collection.)

The Hollingshead Mill Covered Bridge, seen here in 1985, is situated near Catawissa over the Catawissa Creek in Columbia County. The one-span Burr truss bridge was erected in 1850 for $1,180 and named after Henry Hollingshead's Mill. Note the rectangular windows that allow travelers exiting the bridge to see oncoming traffic. (Author's collection.)

Pictured here in 1988, the Stillwater Covered Bridge stretches over Big Fishing Creek south of the village of Stillwater in Columbia County. The 151-foot-long bridge was built in 1849 at a cost of $1,124. The one-span Burr truss design has been closed to roadway traffic since 1949 and serves only pedestrians and bicyclers. Note the unusual slanting sides of the bridge. (Courtesy of Walter W. Pryse.)

Kramer's Covered Bridge is located southwest of Rohrsburg and north of Orangeville in Columbia County. The bridge was built over Mud Run in 1881 at a cost of $414.50. This one-span queen post truss design is 56 feet long. (Author's collection.)

The Wanich Covered Bridge crosses Little Fishing Creek north of Bloomsburg in Columbia County. George Russell Jr. constructed this one-span Burr truss bridge in 1884 at a cost of $505.66. It was named after local farmer John Wanich. Every year during the month of October, Columbia County hosts a Covered Bridge and Arts Festival at Knoebels Amusement Park. (Author's collection.)

The East Paden and West Paden Twin Bridges are located one-fifth of a mile east of Forks in Columbia County. They are Pennsylvania's only surviving twin bridges. Both crossings were built over Huntington Creek by Peter Ent in 1850 for a total cost of $750. The bridges were named after nearby sawmill owner John Paden. One bridge has a Burr truss, and the other has a queen post truss. (Author's collection.)

Knecht's Covered Bridge is two miles northeast of Pleasant Valley, Bucks County. This Springfield Township crossing was constructed in 1873 over Cooks Creek and is supported by a Town truss system, as are all the remaining covered bridges in Bucks County. This photograph was taken on February 14, 1965. (Courtesy of Theodore Burr Covered Bridge Society of Pennsylvania.)

Sheard's Mill Covered Bridge is located east of Quakertown on State Road 4099 in Bucks County. The 1873 bridge crosses Tohickon Creek between Haycock and East Rockhill Townships. This one-span Town truss design still stands next to the mill, which it was named after. The photograph was taken in 1935. (Courtesy of Theodore Burr Covered Bridge Society of Pennsylvania.)

The Uhlerstown Covered Bridge is near the west edge of Uhlerstown in Bucks County. The 1830 Town truss design crosses Tinicum Creek and the 60-mile-long canal towpath of the Delaware Canal. Canal lock No. 18 is located at the bridge. The name "Uhlerstown" comes from Michael Uhler, the owner of a local canal boat-building yard. (Author's collection.)

The Cabin Run Covered Bridge is located on Covered Bridge Road east of Pipersville in Plumstead Township, Bucks County. This one-span Town truss bridge was built in 1874 and crosses Cabin Run Creek. The photograph was taken on July 5, 1962. (Courtesy of Walter W. Pryse.)

The Thomas Mill Covered Bridge, seen here in 1947, crosses Wissahickon Creek in the Chestnut Hill section of northwest Philadelphia. The bridge is located in Fairmount Park along a walking trail. It is the only covered bridge in the United States located within the city limits of a major city. Also, this 1855 Howe truss covered design is only one of five Howe truss covered bridges left in the state of Pennsylvania. Note the sawtooth-edged portal. (Courtesy of Theodore Burr Covered Bridge Society of Pennsylvania.)

The Knox (Valley Forge Dam) Covered Bridge crosses Valley Creek in Valley Forge National Park in Chester County. This is a one-span Burr truss design that was built in 1865 by Robert Russell at a cost of $1,179.99. There was an earlier bridge at this site that was destroyed by a flood. The Knox Covered Bridge is painted white with a wide opening running its length. This photograph was taken in December 1937. (Author's collection.)

This is the Kreidersville (Solt's) Covered Bridge over the Hokendauqua Creek north of Kreidersville in Northampton County. This one-span Burr truss crossing was erected in 1839 and is the only remaining covered bridge in Northampton County. It is closed to traffic but hosts a covered bridge festival every other year. (Author's collection.)

Books (Kauffman's) Covered Bridge was built in 1884 over Sherman's Creek in Jackson Township, Perry County. This one-span Burr truss crossing was one mile southwest of the town of Blain. In this April 18, 1964, photograph, the covered bridge seen here was replaced with a completely new covered bridge in 2003. (Courtesy of Theodore Burr Covered Bridge Society of Pennsylvania.)

Sachs (Sauck's) Covered Bridge, pictured here in 1966, is located five miles southwest of Gettysburg between Cumberland and Freedom Townships in Adams County. Several people believe that the bridge is haunted. During the Civil War, many Union and Confederate soldiers lost their lives near this crossing. Over the years, people have taken photographs in the bridge of what they believe are ghosts of these soldiers, and other people have felt cold spots in the interior. (Courtesy of Walter W. Pryse)

Built in 1865, the Wyit Sprowls Covered Bridge is a one-span queen post truss design in Finley Township, Washington County. In 1998, the bridge was relocated to East Finley Township Park over the Robinson Fork of Wheeling Creek. The Jordan One-Room Schoolhouse, built in 1895, was also moved to the park in 2005. Together, they make a picturesque setting. (Courtesy of Thomas E. Walczak.)

The Longdon Covered Bridge crosses Templeton Fork in West Finley Township, Washington County. This one-span queen post truss crossing is located southwest of West Finley. With a length of 67 feet in the clear, it is one of the longer covered bridges in Washington County. John E. Humphreys took this photograph on June 20, 1963. (Courtesy of Thomas E. Walczak.)

Krepps (County Bridge No. 33) Covered Bridge is located one mile south of Cherry Valley in Mount Pleasant Township, Washington County. This one-span king post truss bridge crosses Raccoon Creek. John E. Humphreys took this photograph on June 21, 1963. (Courtesy of Thomas E. Walczak.)

The Shriver Covered Bridge crosses Hargus Creek in Center Township, Greene County. It is situated on Turkey Hollow Road, approximately two miles south of Rogersville. The one-span queen post truss bridge was built in 1900. (Courtesy of Thomas E. Walczak.)

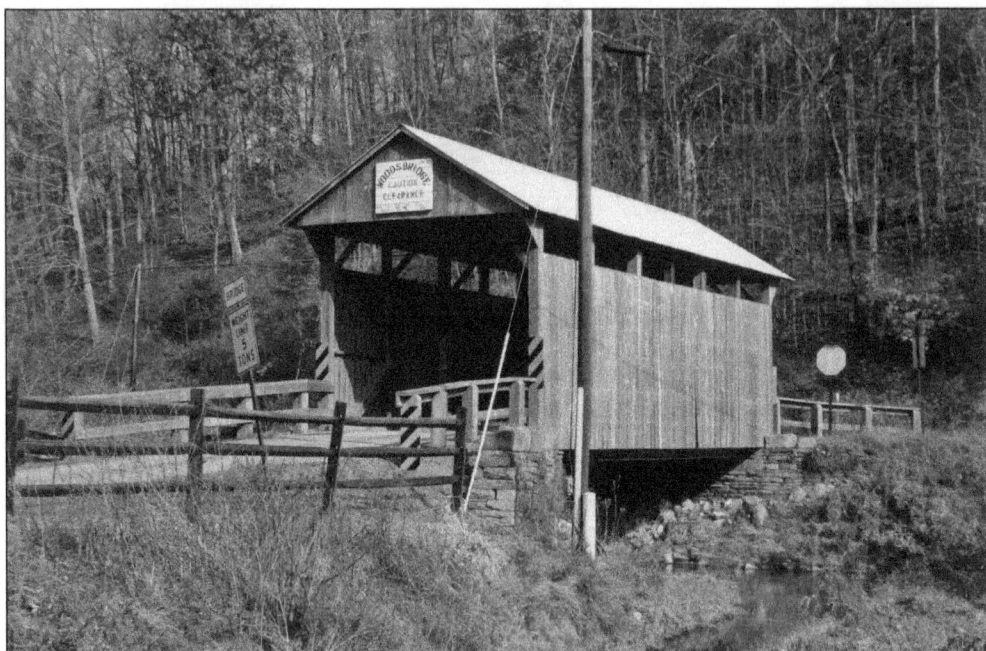

The Neddie Woods (Nettie Woods) Covered Bridge was built in 1882 over Pursley Creek in Center Township, Greene County. The one-span queen post truss crossing is located on Woods Road one mile north of Oak Forest. Edward "Neddie" Woods owned the land at the bridge at the time it was constructed. (Courtesy of Thomas E. Walczak.)

The White Covered Bridge spans Whitely Creek in Greene Township, Greene County. This one-span queen post truss bridge, built in 1919, is located west of Garards Fort near the Washington County line. With a height of 16 feet and 9 inches, it is one of the tallest bridges in the state. Every September, Washington and Greene Counties hold a covered bridge festival. (Courtesy of Thomas E. Walczak.)

Three

PENNSYLVANIA'S RAILROAD COVERED BRIDGES

Only a handful of railroad covered bridges are left in the United States, and there are no railroad covered bridges left in Pennsylvania. Very little information and few photographs exist of these covered bridges. This is a photograph of the Leesport Railroad Covered Bridge near Leesport, Berks County. (Author's collection.)

The Leesport Railroad Covered Bridge crossed the Schuylkill River, a half mile below the town of Leesport. The two-span crossing originally had a roof until it caught on fire from the sparks of a steam engine. The bridge was built in 1872 and was replaced in 1931. This photograph was taken looking west. (Courtesy of George M. Meiser IX.)

This is another view of the Leesport Railroad Covered Bridge, situated just below Leesport near the property of Ontelaunee Orchards. The bridge was on the Moselem Branch of the Reading Railroad. This image was captured from the Leesport side looking downstream. (Courtesy of George M. Meiser IX.)

98

The Virginville Railroad Covered Bridge was erected in 1874 at the lower end of the village of Virginville. The bridge, built by the Reading & Lehigh Railroad, was in existence until 1909. Note that its sides and roof are covered with a type of nonflammable sheet metal. Sparks from engines frequently started fires in wooden bridges. (Courtesy of George M. Meiser IX.)

The Albany Railroad Covered Bridge was constructed in 1874 by the Reading & Lehigh Railroad over the Maiden Creek in Albany Township, Berks County. The two-span railroad bridge was located just below the village of Kempton. In 1914, half of the siding and roof were removed when a train derailed inside of the bridge. (Author's collection.)

Loyal Sock Bridge damaged by flood Jan 5th 1886.

This 1871 railroad bridge was at Montoursville on the Catawissa and Williamsport Branch of the Philadelphia & Reading Railroad. The one-span Howe truss bridge crossed the Loyalsock Creek. The photograph shows the damage caused by an ice jam on January 5, 1886. Nothing is left of the surrounding area but splintered wood, and the covered bridge was left barely standing. The men pictured here review the damage to the railroad tracks. (Courtesy of Theodore Burr Covered Bridge Society of Pennsylvania.)

The Black Railroad Covered Bridge was constructed in 1851 by the Reading Railroad at Mount Carbon in Schuylkill County. It was a one-span Burr truss covered design with two lanes for trains. The covered bridge, which was across the Schuylkill River and Canal, was replaced in 1941. (Courtesy of Schuylkill County Historical Society.)

100

The High Bridge was built on the Schuylkill and Susquehanna Branch of the Philadelphia & Reading Railroad west of Pine Grove in Schuylkill County. This was a Burr truss open-deck railroad covered bridge. Trains traveled on the roof of the bridge while the trusses were protected inside. This crossing existed from the 1850s until the 1940s. (Author's collection.)

This covered railroad bridge was over the Swatara Creek in Pine Grove Township, Schuylkill County. The Burr truss crossing was located about a half mile south of Pine Grove between Blue Mountain and Swatara Hill. This covered bridge was on the Schuylkill & Susquehanna Railroad Branch (Auburn-Pine Grove-Harrisburg) of the Philadelphia & Reading Railroad and was known officially as Reading Company 17/07 Bridge. (Author's collection.)

The Reading Railroad built the Port Clinton Railroad Bridge in 1874 over the Schuylkill River between Berks and Schuylkill Counties. This was a one-span Burr truss railroad design. Note the canal boats that were still using the river when this photograph was taken. Port Clinton was an important center of transportation, with a railroad yard and a center for canal boats to load up with coal from the trains. The covered bridge was replaced in 1909. (Author's collection.)

The Pulpit Rock Twin No. 2 Railroad Covered Bridge, built by the Philadelphia & Reading Railroad in 1842, was located southeast of Port Clinton in Berks County. The name of the bridge comes from the large white stone setting in the Schuylkill River near the right portal of the railroad bridge. (Author's collection.)

The Engleside Railroad Covered Bridge was near Engleside between Lancaster and West Lampeter Townships in Lancaster County. This two-span Howe truss design crossed the Conestoga Creek and featured a length of 279 feet. The covered bridge was built in 1885 and was replaced in 1923. (Courtesy of Theodore Burr Covered Bridge Society of Pennsylvania.)

The Huntington Valley Railroad Covered Bridge was erected near Huntington Valley in Upper Moreland Township in Montgomery County. This one-span covered bridge crossed the Neshaminy Creek and was part of the Reading Railroad. (Courtesy of Richard Sanders Allen.)

The Delphi Railroad Covered Bridge crossed Swamp Creek, situated three-quarters of a mile east of Zeiglersville at Delphi, in Lower Frederick Township, Montgomery County. This Foreman truss covered bridge, which was part of the Perkiomen Branch of the Reading Railroad, was removed in 1910. (Author's collection.)

The Perkiomen Junction Railroad Covered Bridge was built over the Schuylkill River in Montgomery County. This 1868 three-span truss crossing connected Upper Providence Township, Montgomery County, and Schuylkill Township, Chester County. The bridge was on the Perkiomen Branch of the Reading Railroad. (Courtesy of Theodore Burr Covered Bridge Society of Pennsylvania.)

In this close-up view of the Perkiomen Junction Railroad Bridge, the top part of the portal is darkened from the smoke of the train engines. The roof is also missing, most likely having been burned off by sparks from train engines. There is a water barrel next to the right side of the portal of the bridge to help prevent such fires. (Courtesy of Theodore Burr Covered Bridge Society of Pennsylvania.)

Old Covered Bridge at Lewisburg, Pa.

The Lewisburg No. 2 Railroad Covered Bridge was constructed in 1871 over the West Branch of the Susquehanna River between Northumberland and Union Counties at Lewisburg. The bridge was built by the Lewisburg, Tyrone, Spruce Creek & Centre Railroad to serve wagon, trolley, and railroad traffic. (Courtesy of Thomas E. Walczak.)

Scene along the Susquehanna River showing Penna. R. R. and Street Bridge, Lewisburg, Pa.

This image shows seven of the mighty eight spans of the Lewisburg Railroad Bridge. From this photograph, one could assume that the bridge sits high enough to not be touched by high water; however, in 1894, it was damaged by a flood and repaired. Also, in 1899, a flood washed five of the eight spans away, forcing the covered bridge to be rebuilt that same year. By 1902, it was declared unsafe and was demolished by 1910. (Author's collection.)

Columbia Bridge, destroyed by Cyclone, Columbia, Pa.   RICHARDS & ECKMAN

The Columbia-Wrightsville Covered Bridge was the longest covered bridge constructed in the United States. The Howe truss design had 26 spans and stretched 5,390 feet across the Susquehanna River. The first covered bridge at this site, which stood from 1813 to 1832, was destroyed by ice and floodwaters. The second covered bridge, built in 1834, was burned down on June 28, 1863, by the Union army to keep the Confederate army from advancing north. The third covered bridge, which is on both of the postcards seen here, was erected in 1869. (Author's collection.)

No. 5.—Columbia, Pa., Bridge destroyed by cyclone.

This third Columbia-Wrightsville Covered Bridge was built by the Pennsylvania Railroad for both railroad and roadway traffic. It was destroyed on September 30, 1896, by a category 1 hurricane. Note that hurricanes were not given names until the 1950s. This crossing was replaced with an iron bridge. (Author's collection.)

107

This is the Lebanon Valley Railroad Bridge near Buttonwood Street in Reading, Berks County, which crossed the Schuylkill River and the Union Canal. In this photograph of the open-deck railroad design, one can see that trains traveled on the roof while the covered part of the bridge was used to protect the bridge truss. (Courtesy of Historical Society of Berks County.)

The Pine Forge Railroad Bridge carried railroad tracks of the Colebrook Branch of the Reading Railroad over the Manatawny Creek just east of the village of Pine Forge. The stone arch was over a roadway that paralleled the stream. This photograph of the open-deck bridge was taken on May 20, 1940. (Author's collection.)

Four

COVERED BRIDGE
PRESERVATION

This is Siegrist's Mill Covered Bridge in Lancaster County after it was washed off its foundation by a flood in September 2011. Local residents expressed their opinion to have the bridge saved. County commissioners responded that the bridge would be rebuilt, but it could easily have been sold for scrap wood and replaced by a concrete span. People wanted to preserve the past for future generations, so this bridge was given a second life. The photograph was taken on September 20, 2011. (Author's collection.)

This is Kurtz's (Isaac Bear's) Mill Covered Bridge in its original location in Earl Township, Lancaster County, over the Conestoga River. W.W. Upp built this one-span Burr truss crossing in 1876 at a cost of $1,407. A flood washed out the bridge on June 22, 1972. Lancaster County is very active in preserving its covered bridges and realizes their importance in tourism. (Author's collection.)

Kurtz's Mill Bridge was repaired, loaded on a flatbed trailer, and hauled 20 miles away to Lancaster's Central Park in West Lampeter Township. David Esh reconstructed the bridge in the park over Mill Creek in 1974. The total cost of the reconstruction and relocation was about $75,000. The covered bridge now serves park traffic. (Courtesy of Theodore Burr Covered Bridge Society of Pennsylvania.)

In this 1970 photograph is Shearer's Covered Bridge in its original location on South Colebrook Road over Big Chikiswalungo Creek in Lancaster County. The 1856 one-span Burr truss design connected Ralpho and East Hempfield Townships. Because of sharp turns in the road and one-lane traffic over the bridge, the county wanted to replace it with a concrete bridge. (Author's collection.)

In 1971, the county sold Shearer's Bridge to Manheim Borough. The borough had the covered bridge transported to its new location four miles away in Veteran's Memorial Park. Today, the bridge is still over Big Chikiswalungo Creek but is in a quiet park setting and limited to foot and bicycle traffic. (Courtesy of Theodore Burr Covered Bridge Society of Pennsylvania.)

The Fowlersville Covered Bridge was originally constructed near Fowlersville in Columbia County in 1886. The town and bridge were named after the Fowler family, who owned land in the area. Measuring 40 feet in length, the Fowlersville Covered Bridge was originally constructed at a cost of $397 using a queen post truss. It was a convenient truss system to use on short covered bridges. It consisted of a horizontal beam connected to two diagonal beams and uprights. (Courtesy of Theodore Burr Covered Bridge Society of Pennsylvania.)

After being replaced by a concrete bridge in 1986, the Fowlersville Covered Bridge was moved two miles to Brian Creek Park. This photograph of the crossing in its new location was taken in 1988. (Author's collection.)

The Lawrence L. Knoebel Covered Bridge was originally built in 1875 over West Creek north of Benton in Columbia County. In 1937, it was moved about 50 miles to Knoebels Amusement Park near Elysburg. This image was captured before the sidewalk was added to the bridge. (Courtesy of Theodore Burr Covered Bridge Society of Pennsylvania.)

The Lawrence L. Knoebel Bridge is a one-span queen post truss design that crosses Roaring Creek and connects Knoebels Amusement Park and Knoebels campgrounds. This is the site of the annual Covered Bridge and Arts Festival. This photograph was taken in 1988. (Author's collection.)

This was the Colemanville Mill Covered Bridge near Martic Forge in Lancaster County after it was washed out during a flood in 1972—this was not the first time. After each washout, the bridge was rebuilt. James C. Carpenter constructed this one-span Burr truss crossing over the Pequea Creek in 1856 at a cost of $2,244. (Courtesy of Theodore Burr Covered Bridge Society of Pennsylvania.)

In 1992, Lancaster County became proactive and erected a new Colemanville Covered Bridge on abutments five feet higher than the old bridge. Both the old and new bridges were standing when this photograph was taken on August 5, 1992. Today, the new Colemanville Covered Bridge is still standing in southern Lancaster County and has not had a problem with floodwaters. (Author's collection.)

Keller's (Rettew's) Covered Bridge over the Cocalico Creek in Lancaster County had once been on a lightly used backcountry road; however, when this photograph was taken, a housing development had been built next to the bridge. With increased traffic from the housing development, the one-lane 1873 crossing became outdated. In 2006, the county put the covered bridge in storage and replaced it with a new two-lane concrete bridge to handle the increased traffic. This photograph was taken on April 5, 2003. (Author's collection.)

Four years later, Keller's Covered Bridge was taken out of storage and rebuilt over the Cocalico Creek, about one mile upstream from the site of the its original location. The Burr truss covered bridge is once again on a backcountry road serving rural traffic. This photograph was taken during the reconstruction by the author on November 17, 2010. (Author's collection.)

In 2003, the Pool Forge Covered Bridge sat abandoned on a piece of neglected land in Lancaster County. The 1859 Burr truss covered bridge over the Conestoga Creek looked to be rotting away, and no one seemed interested in saving it. This photograph was taken on April 5, 2003. (Author's collection.)

The Historic Pool Forge, Inc., in partnership with the Caernarvon Township supervisors, turned the bridge and surrounding property into a beautiful park. The park now includes, beside the covered bridge, a restored 1700s Ironmasters Mansion, tenant houses, a limekiln, a picnic pavilion, and ball fields. This photograph was taken on May 21, 2011. (Author's collection.)

This is a photograph of the Ebenezer Church and the Ebenezer Church Covered Bridge in its original location over Maple Creek near Ginger Hill in Fallowfield Township, Washington County. This one-span queen post truss bridge had a length of 32 feet. (Courtesy of Theodore Burr Covered Bridge Society of Pennsylvania.)

In the mid-1970s, the Ebenezer Bridge was moved seven miles and reconfigured over the Mingo Creek in Mingo Creek County Park. The bridge was placed on the old abutments of an earlier covered bridge; however, it was too short for the abutments, so steel beams were installed, and part of the siding was extended to reach the abutments. This gives the bridge the appearance of being 18 feet longer than it really is. (Courtesy of Bob Derk.)

The Bartram (William Sager's Gristmill/Lewis Garrett's Mill) Covered Bridge is located west of Newtown Square between Chester and Delaware Counties. Ferdinand Wood built it in 1860 for $1,133. In order to save the bridge, a new concrete bridge bypassed it in 1940. This Crum Creek crossing is closed to traffic and owned by the Marple-Newtown Historical Society. (Courtesy of Theodore Burr Covered Bridge Society of Pennsylvania.)

Jack's Mountain (G. Donald McLaughlin Memorial) Covered Bridge is located 1.5 miles southwest of Fairfield over Toms Creek in Adams County. Joseph Smith constructed the one-span Burr truss bridge in 1890. Today, the crossing is located along a busy road, and instead of replacing it with a new two-lane concrete bridge, traffic lights were installed to control the flow of traffic. At the time the photograph was taken on April 18, 2004, the lights were working quite well. (Author's collection.)

This is Wertz's Covered Bridge over the Tulpehocken Creek near Reading, Berks County. Note that the bridge is leaning to the right. There are also some dilapidated lower beams, rotten arch ends, and several scarf joints that are becoming separated; the bridge also bows downstream, and a center diagonal beam is broken. Something had to be done to save it from collapsing into the creek. In 1984, the bridge was restored at a cost of $212,224. This photograph was taken in 1983. (Author's collection.)

In 1984, after the roof, floor, and siding were removed, Wertz's Bridge was jacked up on scaffolding to take the weight off all the wooden members. This allowed the workmen to work on the truss without any pressure on the joints. (Author's collection.)

One of Wertz's center diagonal beams of the main king post shown in this June 7, 1984, photograph was broken in 1959 when it was hit by a car. This broken diagonal beam had to be removed, and a new diagonal beam had to be cut and inserted in its place. (Author's collection.)

In this image, one of the scarf joints of the lower chord became separated, and the wood started cracking. This was another major concern. This scarf joint had to be replaced, and then the joint had to be tightened up. This photograph was taken on June 7, 1984. (Author's collection.)

In this photograph, the arches appear rotted at their ends. The rotted wood was cut out to be filled in with concrete. It can be seen from the large block of concrete on the right that this was not the first time ends of the arches were replaced with concrete. This image was captured on August 22, 1984. (Author's collection.)

The work of the restoration of Wertz's Bridge that began in June 1984 was finished in November of the same year. The crossing pictured here has white undercoating and awaits a coat of red paint. Today, Wertz's Bridge is open to pedestrian and bicycle traffic only and has been given a new future. It is the longest single-span covered bridge in Pennsylvania and the second-longest single-span covered bridge in the United States. This photograph was taken on June 17, 1985. (Author's collection.)

The Pleasantville Covered Bridge in Pleasantville, Berks County, was closed to traffic in 1993 because of a collapsed stone wing wall. A decision needed to be made to either replace the bridge with a new concrete crossing or to restore and keep the one-lane covered bridge. After being closed for nine years, the decision was made to restore it. This was to be a complete restoration, using as much of the original wood as possible. This photograph was taken on July 4, 1995. (Author's collection.)

Work began on the Pleasantville Bridge in 2002, as pictured here on August 30, 2002. After removing the sides, the roof, and the floor on August 30, the two trusses were moved intact to an adjacent field where they and other parts of the bridge would be worked on over the next 21 months at a cost of $2.2 million. (Author's collection.)

The collapsed wing wall of the Pleasantville Bridge was completely dug out and replaced with a new wing wall made of concrete with a stone facing. Work on the bridge was done year-round. In this winter photograph, work was done by using heated blowers and plastic sheeting to cure the concrete. This photograph was taken on January 7, 2003, when temperatures were around 19 degrees Fahrenheit. (Author's collection.)

On June 25, 2003, four steel I-beams were delivered and put in place. These I-beams would be completely hidden after the covered bridge was built around them. The span would support its own weight while the weight of traffic going over would be placed on the I-beams. This photograph was taken on June 30, 2003. (Author's collection.)

The truss pieces were laid out on the ground. Original pieces that could be salvaged were used, and rotten timbers were replaced with new pieces of timber brought in from the state of Washington. In this June 30, 2003, photograph, a new upper chord on the right is being prepared to be cut so it will match the rotten chord on the left. (Author's collection.)

The first restored truss of the Pleasantville Bridge is being lowered back into place onto the abutment shelf on October 29, 2003. It took two hours to get this truss into place because some adjustments had to be made. (Author's collection.)

124

The redone abutment walls and main truss of the Pleasantville Bridge are completed and waiting installation of the floor, roof, and sides. This image, taken on January 7, 2004, is one of over 600 photographs taken by the author during the restoration of this bridge. (Author's collection.)

The finished Pleasantville Covered Bridge is shown here after 21 months of restoration. The bridge looks new and can handle several tons of weight. This photograph was taken on May 10, 2004. This and other bridges in this chapter have been saved for future generations to enjoy thanks to people getting involved in saving these vital links to the past. (Author's collection.)

BIBLIOGRAPHY

Allen, Richard Sanders. *Covered Bridges of the Middle Atlantic States.* Brattleboro, VT: The Stephen Greene Press, 1959.

Evans, Benjamin D. and June R. *Pennsylvania's Covered Bridges.* Pittsburgh, PA: University of Pittsburgh Press, 2001.

Gill, Paul E. *Drive the Road and Bridge the Ford Highway Bridges of 19th-Century Cumberland County.* Camp Hill, PA: Plank's Suburban Press, Inc., 1992.

James, Arthur E. *Covered Bridges of Chester County, Pennsylvania.* Kennett Square, PA: KNA Press, Inc., 1976.

Kipphorn, Thomas G. *The Covered Bridges of Lancaster County, Pennsylvania, 1800–1987.* The Compiler, 1987.

Moll, Fred J. *Covered Bridges of Berks County, Pennsylvania.* Reading, PA: Reading Eagle Publishing Company, 2001.

———. *Pennsylvania's Covered Bridges-Our Heritage.* Reading, PA: Reading Eagle Press, 2004.

———. *Pleasantville Covered Bridge Restoration.* Hamburg, PA: Windsor Press, 2004.

———. *Pennsylvania's Historic Bridges.* Mount Pleasant, SC: Arcadia Publishing, 2007.

———. *Theodore Burr Covered Bridge Society of Pennsylvania 50th Anniversary Book.* Boyertown, PA: Boyertown Press, 2008.

Theodore Burr Covered Bridge Society of Pennsylvania. *Portals Magazines.* Vol. 5, No. 2– Vol. 9, No. 1.

ABOUT THE
ORGANIZATION

The purpose of the society is to promote the preservation and restoration of the remaining historical covered bridges in the Commonwealth of Pennsylvania through educational programs for the members, as well as for the public at large, for the interest and enjoyment of all, as well as succeeding generations. Visit us at www.tbcbspa.com.

Visit us at
arcadiapublishing.com